LEVEL
**3**

# What Is an Archaeologist?

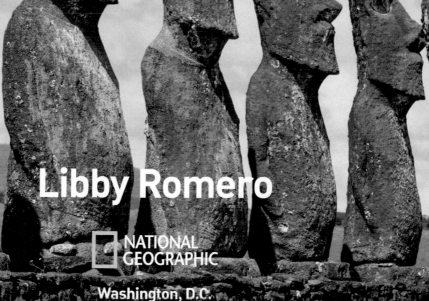

## Libby Romero

**NATIONAL GEOGRAPHIC**

Washington, D.C.

# For the Mossey girls —L. R.

Designed by YAY! Design

Library of Congress Cataloging-in-Publication Data
Names: Romero, Libby, author.
Title: National Geographic readers : what is an archaeologist? / by Libby Romero.
Other titles: What is an archaeologist?
Description: Washington, DC : National Geographic Kids, [2019] | Series: National Geographic readers | Audience: Grades K-3. | Audience: Ages 6-9.
Identifiers: LCCN 2018057777 (print) | LCCN 2018058696 (ebook) | ISBN 9781426335136 (e-book) | ISBN 9781426335143 (e-book + audio) | ISBN 9781426335112 (pbk.) | ISBN 9781426335129 (hardcover)
Subjects: LCSH: Archaeologists--Juvenile literature. | Archaeology--Juvenile literature.
Classification: LCC CC107 (ebook) | LCC CC107 .R66 2019 (print) | DDC 930.1--dc23
LC record available at https://lccn.loc.gov/2018057777

The author and publisher gratefully acknowledge the content review of this book by Debora Trein, program officer, Human Journey, National Geographic Society, and the literacy review of this book by Mariam Jean Dreher, professor of reading education, University of Maryland, College Park.

## Author's Note

The word "archaeology" comes from the Greek word *arkhaios*, which means "ancient." Archaeology became a field of scientific study about 150 years ago. But people have been digging things up for thousands of years. They wanted to understand the mysteries people before them had left behind. One mystery that still hasn't been solved can be found on Easter Island (or Rapa Nui), Polynesia, pictured on the title page. Long ago, people there built about 900 giant stone statues called moai. Nobody knows how or why the islanders carved them.

On the table of contents page, the artifact pictured is a Native American arrowhead.

**Photo Credits**
AS=Alamy Stock Photo; GI=Getty Images; NGIC=National Geographic Image Collection; SS=Shutterstock

Cover, Manami Yahata/NGIC; header (throughout), Noch/SS; vocabulary art (throughout), Denis Gorelkin/SS;1, Viktor Gmyria/Dreamstime; 3, Stephanie Frey/SS; 4-5, Erika Larsen/NGIC; 6-7, Kenneth Garrett/NGIC; 8, Gordon Wiltsie/NGIC; 9, imageBROKER/SS; 10, Jericho (gouache on paper)/Private Collection/© Look and Learn/Bridgeman Images; 11, arhendrix/SS; 12, O. Louis Mazzatenta/NGIC; 13, Adrian Dennis/AFP/GI; 14, Andrey Armyagov/SS; 15 (INSET), DigitalGlobe/GI; 15, DigitalGlobe/GI; 16, Blue Media/National Geographic; 17, Stephen Barnes/AS; 18, Keith Seramur; 19, ITAR-TASS News Agency/AS; 20, Courtesy of Sarah Parcak/Cengage/NGIC; 21, Universal History Archive/UIG/SS; 22, Paul Nicklen/NGIC; 23, Don Couch/Barcroft Media/GI; 24, Constanza Ceruti/Society of Woman Geographers; 25 (LE), Robert Harding Picture Library/NGIC; 25 (RT), Abid Mehmood/NGIC; 26 (UP), starmaro/SS; 26 (CTR), Matthias Hiekel/EPA/SS; 26 (LO), photoDISC; 27 (UP LE), Vlad Ghiea/AS; 27 (UP RT), Bill Curtsinger/NGIC; 27 (LO LE), Francisco Juarez/NGIC; 27 (LO RT), agnormark/GI; 28, Universal History Archive/UIG via GI; 29 (UP), Taylor Kennedy/Sitka Productions/NGIC; 29 (LO), Jarno Gonzalez Zarraonandia/SS; 30 (UP), James P. Blair/NGIC; 30 (LO), Spencer Sutton/Science Source; 31, O. Louis Mazzatenta/NGIC; 32, Dan Wallace/Dreamstime; 33 (UP), Dave Yoder/NGIC; 33 (LO), Gregory A. Harlin/NGIC; 34, duncan1890/GI; 35 (UP), Rui Vieira/AS; 35 (LO), Peter Corns/AP Images; 36, Joe McNally/NGIC; 37, Universal History Archive/UIG/SS; 39, William Albert Allard/NGIC; 40, John Moore/GI; 41, Robert Harding Picture Library/NGIC; 42, Bill Ballenberg/NGIC; 43, Ozkan Bilgin/Anadolu Agency/GI; 44 (UP), Kenneth Garrett/NGIC; 44 (CTR UP), Marcio Jose Bastos Silva/SS; 44 (CTR LE), James P. Blair/NGIC; 44 (CTR RT), Jennifer White Maxwell/SS; 44 (CTR LO), Don Mammoser/SS; 44 (LO), Kichigin/SS; 45 (UP), Bethany Peterson/NGIC; 45 (CTR LE), Guillermo Pruneda/NGIC; 45 (CTR RT), Blue Media/National Geographic; 45 (LO UP), DeA Picture Library/Granger.com - All rights reserved; 45 (LO LE), Jaroslav Moravcik/SS; 45 (LO RT), Paul Nicklen/NGIC; 45 (LO LO), Cedric Weber/SS; 46 (UP), The Washington Post/GI; 46 (CTR LE), Paul Nicklen/NGIC; 46 (CTR RT), Vacclav/Dreamstime; 46 (LO LE), ITAR-TASS News Agency/AS; 46 (LO RT), DigitalGlobe/GI; 47 (UP LE), Hulton-Deutsch Collection/Corbis/Corbis via GI; 47 (UP RT), W. Scott McGill/SS; 47 (CTR LE), Erika Larsen/NGIC; 47 (CTR RT), Gordon Wiltsie/NGIC; 47 (LO LE), Wes C. Skiles/NGIC; 47 (LO RT), Todd Buchanan/NGIC

**National Geographic supports K–12 educators with ELA Common Core Resources. Visit natgeoed.org/commoncore for more information.**

# Table of Contents

# What Is Archaeology?

Have you ever wanted to travel back through time? Discover lost cities? Or find a sunken ship filled with gold? Treasure hunters do it all the time in the movies. And lots of times, their characters are archaeologists (AR-kee-OL-uh-jists).

A team of archaeologists works at Nunalleq in Alaska, U.S.A. They're searching for objects from the Yupik people from the 1660s. More than 2,500 objects have been found. There may be many more.

In real life, archaeologists go on these kinds of adventures, too. But these scientists aren't treasure hunters or time travelers. They are more like detectives—their job is to solve mysteries. Their mission is to understand how people lived in the past.

## Word to Know

**ARCHAEOLOGIST:** A scientist who studies objects to learn how people in specific times and places lived

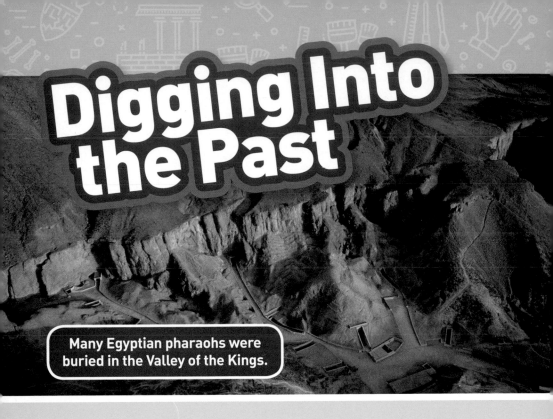

# Digging Into the Past

Many Egyptian pharaohs were buried in the Valley of the Kings.

Archaeologists solve mysteries about the past by looking for clues. These clues can be objects that people made and used, called artifacts. Clues can also be letters and documents, or buildings people lived in.

But clues aren't always easy to find. So, archaeologists study old maps and read ancient stories. They also look at photos taken from space. This helps them spot possible sites they can't see from the ground.

# Finding King Tut

In 1922, British archaeologist Howard Carter went to Egypt. He studied the landscape and watched how it changed when it rained. This led him to the most likely places to find long-buried tombs. And in one of those places, he discovered the most famous find of the 20th century. Carter found the 3,000-year-old tomb of Egyptian pharaoh Tutankhamun, or King Tut.

## Words to Know

**ARTIFACT:** A portable object made or modified by humans

**SITE:** Any place where there are remains of human activity

Making a grid helps archaeologists keep track of the clues they find.

Once a site is located, archaeologists divide the area into a grid. They use the grid to make a map. Then they use the map to record the exact location of everything they find.

Then, very slowly and carefully, they begin to search. They look for features and artifacts that people left behind. When they find something, they take photos. They also draw pictures and make detailed notes. They send artifacts back to the lab so they can study them later.

Archaeologists take photos of all artifacts and the area around where they found them.

## Words to Know

**GRID:** A series of connected squares or rectangles

**FEATURE:** A human-made structure that cannot be moved, like a wall or a floor

Like any good detective, archaeologists want to find the truth. And sometimes they find new clues that prove earlier ideas were wrong. That's what British archaeologist Kathleen Kenyon did.

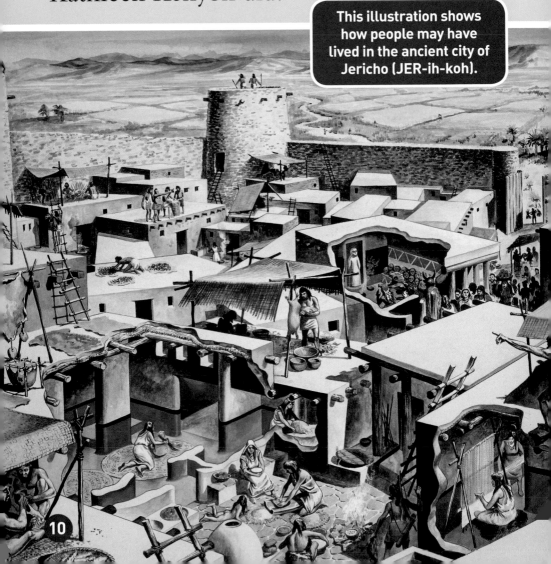

This illustration shows how people may have lived in the ancient city of Jericho (JER-ih-koh).

Kenyon created a new way to dig for and find the age of artifacts discovered at a site. She used this idea when she explored the Middle Eastern city of Jericho. She proved that the ancient city was destroyed 1,550 years earlier than people had thought.

## Reading the Soil

The ground under you shows periods of time. Soil builds up in layers over many years. As each layer gets covered up, clues from that time period get buried, too. Kathleen Kenyon wanted to see how the layers fit together. So she dug trenches to make a grid in the ground. Studying the layers of soil in the trench walls helped her figure out when things actually happened.

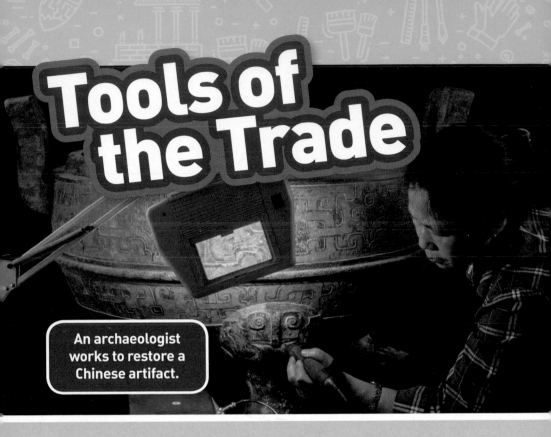

# Tools of the Trade

An archaeologist works to restore a Chinese artifact.

Archaeologists don't actually spend all of their time digging for artifacts. Their field season may only be a few weeks or months long. They spend more time in the lab, studying everything they've collected.

In the field, modern archaeologists collect artifacts they find on the surface. They try to dig as little as possible. Digging disturbs sites and destroys important clues.

# Inside an Archaeologist's Tool Kit

On site, archaeologists use some simple tools that you can probably find in your own home. This includes tape measures, toothbrushes, brooms, and dustpans. They also use dental picks, like the ones the dentist uses to clean your teeth. Their most important tool is a trowel. Masons use these flat-bladed tools to lay bricks. Archaeologists use trowels to carefully remove thin layers of soil.

trowel

## Word to Know

**FIELD SEASON:** A period of time when an archaeologist works on site, or "in the field"

13

Luckily, today's archaeologists have a lot of cool tools to help them find answers in other ways. One of those tools is satellite imagery. These photos help archaeologists search large areas more quickly.

## Word to Know

**SATELLITE IMAGERY:** Photos taken by satellites in space

How? Archaeologists pick one area in a satellite photo and zoom in to see it up close. Sometimes they spot unusual patterns on the ground. Other times they may see areas that reflect light in different ways. These clues could show where something is buried.

The ancient city of Dura-Europos, on the bank of the Euphrates River in Syria, is more than 2,000 years old. The many holes seen in a close-up view of the satellite photo (inset) show where robbers have damaged the site.

At this Maya city called Tikal, archaeologists used LiDAR to make a map of the land. LiDAR digitally removed thick plants and trees to show the ancient ruins below.

To get a closer look, archaeologists can use remote sensing from the ground and from the air. From an airplane, helicopter, or drone, they shoot a laser beam at the ground. That beam is part of a tool called LiDAR, or Light Detection and Ranging.

A LiDAR machine has a laser, a scanner, and a GPS, which finds a location from a satellite. When the laser hits the ground, beams of light bounce back from the surface. The scanner records GPS readings from each hit and makes a 3D map of the area.

## Paving the Way

Ground penetrating radar (GPR) was one of the first remote sensing technologies. It is used on the ground to help archaeologists search without digging. GPR sends radio signals into the ground. The signals bounce back when they hit something. How long it takes for the signals to bounce back can tell archaeologists how deeply something is buried.

## Word to Know

REMOTE SENSING: Technology used to detect clues that we can't see with just our eyes, or that are hidden underground

On the ground, archaeologists use other remote sensing tools. To find buried stone walls, they use electricity. They stick a grid of long, thin probes into the ground. Then they send electricity through the probes. Electricity moves more easily through some materials than others. This helps them locate structures buried almost five feet deep.

probe

Archaeologists use the information they get from probes like these to map the ground. This helps them figure out where things are buried.

A handheld x-ray tool can tell what is in glass, ceramic, and metal materials.

To look for signs of ancient objects burned by fire, archaeologists use magnets. Burned objects leave magnetic traces in the soil. Archaeologists use a tool called a magnetometer to look for the traces. Areas with high readings could be ditches where ancient people burned objects long ago.

**Word to Know**

**TRACE:** Evidence of something from the past, often in very small amounts

19

# Archaeologists in Action

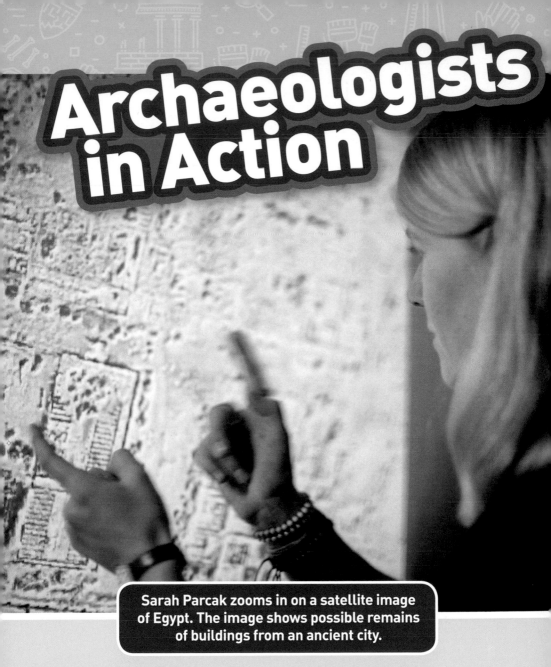

Sarah Parcak zooms in on a satellite image of Egypt. The image shows possible remains of buildings from an ancient city.

Today's archaeologists can explore the world like never before. Sarah Parcak explores Earth from 400 miles above its surface. She's a space archaeologist.

## It Takes All Kinds

There are lots of different types of archaeologists. For example, experimental archaeologists use the tools and technology people had in the past to make copies of things they used. In 1947, a man built a copy of a large raft called the *Kon-Tiki*. He sailed it from South America to Polynesia to prove that ancient people could have done the same thing.

Parcak doesn't really go into space. She uses satellite imagery and other tools to do her work. She's helped find 17 possible pyramids; 3,100 forgotten settlements; and 1,000 lost tombs. She even created a website where people can review satellite imagery. They tell Parcak where they think sites are located. Then she checks the images to see if sites are really there.

Underwater archaeologist Guillermo de Anda needs a wet suit and oxygen tank to do his job. More often than not, his site is in a cave or cenote (seh-NO-teh).

Guillermo de Anda at work near Yucatán, Mexico

De Anda studies the Maya civilization. He and his team are exploring the caves, tunnels, and cenotes beneath the Yucatán Peninsula in Mexico. They are making a 3D map of the area. They hope to find out how this underwater network is connected to the Maya pyramids above.

**Q** What do archaeologists say when it's time to eat dinner?

**A** "Dig in."

## Word to Know

**CENOTE:** A sinkhole or a cave that is filled with water

Guillermo de Anda can spend up to seven hours a day in the water exploring caves and cenotes.

Constanza Ceruti goes to great heights to study ancient cultures. She is a high-altitude archaeologist. She and anthropologist Johan Reinhard discovered the best preserved mummies ever found. They were on top of a 22,100-foot-tall volcano in Argentina.

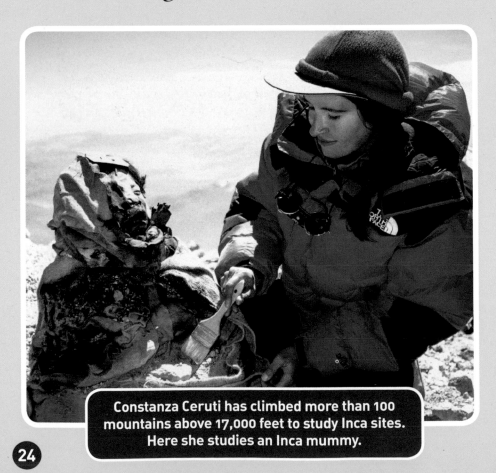

Constanza Ceruti has climbed more than 100 mountains above 17,000 feet to study Inca sites. Here she studies an Inca mummy.

Kalash headgear

Sayed Gul Kalash is the first Kalash archaeologist and the only Kalash woman trained as a scientist.

For archaeologist Sayed Gul Kalash, the work is more personal. She wants to preserve her culture. Gul Kalash is one of the 3,500 remaining Kalash people in Pakistan. She searches for artifacts that tell stories about her culture.

**Word to Know**

ANTHROPOLOGIST: A scientist who studies human behavior, culture, and development

# 7 TYPES OF Archaeologists

**1** Prehistorical archaeologists study civilizations that did not have a writing system.

Historical archaeologists study cultures that left behind written records. They study the records to learn more about the past. **2**

**3** Classical archaeologists study ancient Greece and Rome.

**4** Egyptologists study the history and culture of Egypt.

Underwater archaeologists work in rivers, lakes, wetlands, and the ocean. They search for things like shipwrecks and submerged cities.

**5**

**6** Environmental archaeologists study how changes in the environment affected ancient people's lives.

Garbologists are archaeologists who study what people throw away. They dig through garbage to identify patterns and changes in people's habits.

**7**

# Unexpected Discoveries

Believe it or not, some of the greatest artifacts ever found were discovered by accident. For example, in 1799, French soldiers building a fort in Egypt dug up the Rosetta Stone.

The Rosetta Stone is a granite stone with the same text in three languages: Greek, an ancient Egyptian script, and Egyptian hieroglyphs. People used the stone to figure out what hieroglyphs meant.

In 1947, a shepherd in Israel threw a rock into a cave and discovered the Dead Sea Scrolls. And in China, in 1974, a farmer digging a well uncovered the first of thousands of terra-cotta warriors. The statues are more than 2,000 years old.

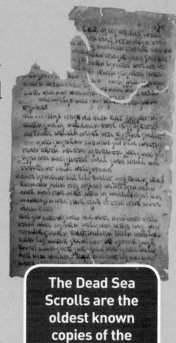

The Dead Sea Scrolls are the oldest known copies of the Hebrew Bible.

The terra-cotta army contains more than 7,000 life-size clay soldiers, horses, and chariots. The warriors were created for the first emperor of China.

In recent years, archaeologists have used technology to make new discoveries about old finds. The

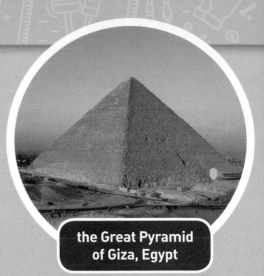

the Great Pyramid of Giza, Egypt

Great Pyramid of Giza is a good example. Using new laser technology, archaeologists tracked the movement of tiny particles that traveled through the stone and air. They discovered a large hidden space in the middle of the pyramid.

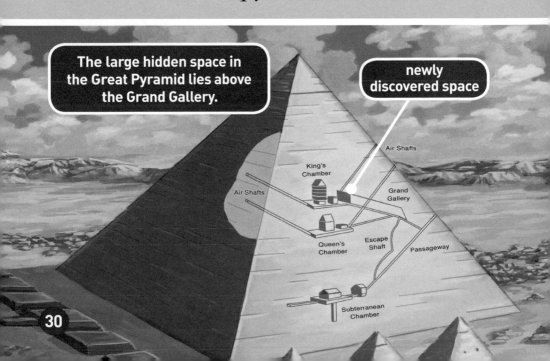

The large hidden space in the Great Pyramid lies above the Grand Gallery.

newly discovered space

Air Shafts

King's Chamber

Air Shafts

Grand Gallery

Queen's Chamber

Escape Shaft

Passageway

Subterranean Chamber

Technology has helped archaeologists learn more about the ancient Roman site of Pompeii, too. In 2018, archaeologists began exploring the city with laser scanners and drones. They found shops, gardens, art, and homes that had not been known before.

Pompeii, Italy, was buried and preserved by ash and rock when Mount Vesuvius erupted in A.D. 79.

Angkor Wat, Cambodia

Angkor Wat is the largest religious monument in the world. Archaeologists have studied the area around the temple for more than 100 years. But recently, a team explored the nearby jungle with LiDAR. In just two weeks, they found the remains of more temples, roads, and waterways. They found new "suburbs." The ancient city of Angkor was bigger and more advanced than anyone had expected.

# New Science, Old Site

One site in the rainforest in Honduras had been known by local people for centuries. Their ancestors had built amazing cities there. But the cities weren't known to outside scientists. In 2012, filmmakers used LiDAR to scan the area. They noticed patterns. A team of experts searched the area on foot. They found the remains of ancient temples, roads, and waterways—and thousand-year-old artifacts!

site showing trees

site with trees removed by LiDAR

PLAZA

TERRACES

449 ft
(137 m)

LiDAR scan showing ancient ruins

an artist's drawing of the site

# Unsolved Mysteries

New tools have helped archaeologists solve age-old mysteries. For example, in 1485, England's King Richard III died in battle. People later demolished the church where he was buried. Over time, they forgot where the church had been. England couldn't find its king!

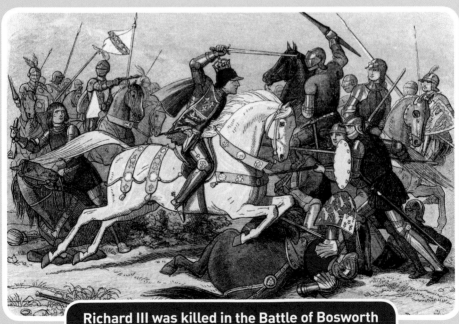

Richard III was killed in the Battle of Bosworth Field, shown in this illustration.

In 2012, archaeologists compared old maps to new ones. They found his grave under a parking lot in Leicester (LESS-ter), England. Whose burial site will archaeologists find next? Alexander the Great? Or maybe Genghis Khan?

Archaeologist Claire Graham uses GPR to search for Richard III's lost grave.

The discovered grave was small, shallow, and had rounded sides. Archaeologists say this means Richard III was buried in a hurry.

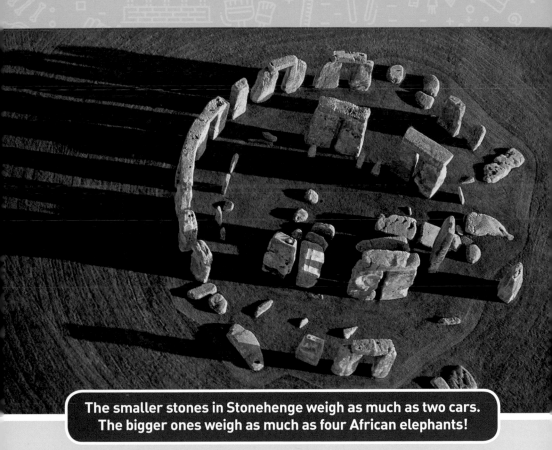

**The smaller stones in Stonehenge weigh as much as two cars. The bigger ones weigh as much as four African elephants!**

Some great mysteries are impossible to miss. Stonehenge in southern England is a good example. It took people more than 1,000 years to make this prehistoric monument out of giant stones. How did they do it? And why? Nobody knows . . . yet. Stonehenge could have been a calendar, a place of healing, or even a temple to sun or moon gods.

# The Unreadable Book

The Voynich manuscript, discovered in 1912, is a book that nobody can read. Experts think this 600-year-old book might be about science or magic. It contains lots of illustrations. But the words on its 250 pages are written in a language that nobody has ever seen before.

Another mystery hidden in plain sight is the Nasca lines in the desert in Peru. In the late 1920s, airplanes first flew over the desert. People saw that the lines were actually giant pictures. There are many ideas, but nobody is sure why the Nasca people made these lines or what they mean.

Some mysteries might not be real. Ancient Greeks described Atlantis as a great island that sank into the sea more than 10,000 years ago. Do you think Atlantis is real? It may not be, but there are many more mysteries waiting to be solved!

The Nasca lines are about 2,000 years old. Some are giant lines. Others look like plants or animals, like this spider figure.

# The Future of Archaeology

Archaeology may deal with the past, but new high-tech tools are taking it into the future. People are curious. They want to know what happened and why. Figuring that out is easier now than ever before.

But sometimes, archaeologists don't have enough time to do their work. In some places, their sites are disappearing. Robbers steal artifacts. Sites are destroyed in wars or knocked down to build new things. Other sites are affected by nature.

This hole in Bamiyan, Afghanistan, is where the world's largest standing Buddha used to be.

Before it was destroyed by war, the Buddha statue had existed for 1,700 years.

Archaeologists work at an ancient site in Lambayeque Valley, Peru.

Protecting these sites is important. So is finding people who know how to uncover their secrets. If you're interested in helping out, check with your local historical society, national park service, or library. Then dig in! One day, you might uncover ancient mysteries!

# Want to Be an Archaeologist?

Here are some tips to get started:

1. Observe: Pick a place and look around. Draw a map and take notes describing what you see.

2. Be curious: How did people use this place 10 years ago? Or 100? Ask your family or neighbors. Go to the library to learn more.

3. Explore: Go to new places. Learn about the world around you.

4. Study: Archaeologists study all types of science, history, languages, and cultures. Pick an area you are interested in. Read and find out more.

5. Be responsible: If you find a possible artifact, leave it where it is and tell a grown-up. You may have found a new clue from the past!

# QUIZ WHIZ

How much do you know about archaeologists? After reading this book, probably a lot! Take this quiz and find out.

Answers are at the bottom of page 45.

**1**

### What do archaeologists study?

A. the past
B. the present
C. the future
D. space

**2**

### Which of these could be an artifact?

A. a pyramid
B. a dinosaur fossil
C. a tool
D. a home

### Kathleen Kenyon studied _____ of soil to better understand time.

A. piles
B. shapes
C. traces
D. layers

**3**

**4**

**What can a magnetometer do?**

A. explore with laser scanners
B. locate traces of burned objects
C. find stone walls
D. show time and location

_____ can make 3D maps of land on the surface of Earth.

A. Features
B. GPR
C. LiDAR
D. A handheld x-ray tool

**5**

**6**

**Where does Guillermo de Anda search for artifacts?**

A. from space
B. underwater
C. on top of mountains
D. in Pakistan

**Which of these mysteries are archaeologists still trying to solve?**

A. Where is King Tut buried?
B. When was Jericho destroyed?
C. What is a cenote?
D. What was Stonehenge?

**7**

Answers: 1. A, 2. C, 3. D, 4. B, 5. C, 6. B, 7. D

# Glossary

**ANTHROPOLOGIST:** A scientist who studies human behavior, culture, and development

**CENOTE:** A sinkhole or a cave that is filled with water

**FEATURE:** A human-made structure that cannot be moved, like a wall or a floor

**REMOTE SENSING:** Technology used to detect clues that we can't see with just our eyes, or that are hidden underground

**SATELLITE IMAGERY:** Photos taken by satellites in space

**ARCHAEOLOGIST:** A scientist who studies objects to learn how people in specific times and places lived

**ARTIFACT:** A portable object made or modified by humans

**FIELD SEASON:** A period of time when an archaeologist works on site, or "in the field"

**GRID:** A series of connected squares or rectangles

**SITE:** Any place where there are remains of human activity

**TRACE:** Evidence of something from the past, often in very small amounts

# Index